The Politics of Disability

A Guide for Men

-Peter Wright-

Copyright © 2015 by Disability-Press

Table of Contents

Preface

In recent years the disability sector has seen the rise of political ideologies directing the provision of services and supports to disabled persons; Marxist, radical feminist, and social justice extremism being the more obvious among them. Such imposed frameworks have important implications for the quality of care received by service users, and to whom services might be tailored, though few academics have acknowledged their impact on men with disabilities.

As we describe in the following pages the negative impact of such ideologies is disproportionally borne by male service users whose experiences and needs are often neglected. We describe some of the more problematic issues and offer positive suggestions for men to both identify and hopefully navigate their way around these biases.

The first chapter by independent researcher Hannah Wallen looks at recent feminist advocacy for people with disabilities, which amounts to a *gendering* of what are essentially genderless issues. The result of such gendering is to exclude men from important service considerations, a selective practice that amounts to an attack on men's civil rights.

The subsequent three chapters by Peter Wright were first published in 2015 at the Men's Mental Health Network which have been updated for this volume. These essays explore the experience of men with disabilities living in a world that often fails to meet reasonable expectations, particularly in areas of provision of care, and protections against violence and abuse. The articles discuss possible reasons for these failures, in particular the creep of gynocentric attitudes in the disability sector, while offering positive encouragement for men to self-advocate, where possible, in their own best interest.

Peter Wright, December 5, 2015

Chapter 1:
Gendering disability rights

The feminists of the organization behind the recent Women's March say feminists seek to break barriers faced by the disabled. Their description is a long-form rundown of conditions needed for disabled individuals to live as a healthy, safe and secure part of their community.

That sounds like a noble goal, one that the disabilities advocacy and care community has worked toward for generations. It would be nice to have feminists catch up to that *after generations of association between their movement and eugenics.*

Feminist eugenicists have always been all for disability rights, except… you know, any kind of right to be protected during gestation, arguably the most vulnerable time in a human life, or the right to not have one's bodily autonomy violated via forced sterilization, or the right to have one's existence treated as legitimate rather than as nature's horrible mistake.

Margaret Sanger, founder of the American Birth Control League, which later became Planned Parenthood, was a staunch proponent of aborting unborn babies believed to be handicapped, and involuntary sterilization of the intellectually disabled. That attitude was carried through decades of feminists, to Ruth Bader Ginsburg telling Sunday New York Times Magazine reporter Emily Bazelon, "Frankly I had thought that at the time Roe was decided, there was concern about population growth and particularly growth in populations that we don't want to have too many of."

There's a human rights focus for you… such compassion!

Of course, that's just the feminist eugenicists, right? Remember, feminism is not a monolith.

Well, except when it comes to the way feminism's Patriarchy Theory bleeds all over the greater human rights advocacy community.

Three years ago, I examined an article published on time.com. It said violence against disabled women was being ignored in several countries. As I dug through the story's references, I found a disturbing pattern: Feminist-led research by or cited by Human Rights Watch, the organization cited in the article, was documenting discrimination and other issues faced by disabled people of both sexes, including abuse and lack of access to medical care, but reporting as if women were uniquely targeted and uniquely impacted.

Various reports interpreted a lack of facilities dedicated strictly to serving women, overall low quality or availability of service regardless of the helpseeker's sex, or the lack of abortion services in countries where abortion is illegal, all as discrimination against or neglect of disabled women. Instances of men being similarly disadvantaged did not receive the same treatment.

Human Rights watch applied the same bias to research on sexual violence, reporting on prevalence data on the use of rape as a war weapon, which recorded victims of both sexes, as if it is used strictly against women. This is important to this topic due to the fact that disability increases the individual's vulnerability to all abuses, including sexual violence.

Further examination of their research on violence indicated that Human Rights watch is using two other common feminist techniques for avoiding information that contradicts the victims-must-be-female part of their narrative. One is only looking into women's experiences of genderless issues, and then reporting their findings as a women's issue. The other is attributing women's adverse experiences to being targeted due to their gender, but not attributing the same adverse experiences to gender when men report them. Through that filter every disadvantage any women face becomes a women's issue, but no disadvantages faced by men are treated as men's issues.

Meanwhile, in the US where feminists have been active for a hundred years, there are services for the disabled that are reserved strictly for women. This includes government initiatives like the Health and Human Services department's website womenshealth.gov's page on violence against women with disabilities, which provides information and links to resources for disabled women and their families. Want similar information for men with disabilities?

A cursory look at menshealth.gov revealed that there are several interesting advertisements, articles, and other publications related to men's health, all of which were listed on the landing page my internet service provider shows when you try to visit a website that doesn't exist, but has "men's health" in the url.

So of course, there's no page on violence against men with disabilities at that address, despite the fact that, as reported by the Vera institute of Justice, Men with disabilities experience victimization, including sexual violence, at rates higher than men without disabilities… which means their disabilities *are* making them vulnerable to abuse, and not enough is being done to counteract that vulnerability.

Oh, but Uncle Sam isn't completely devoid of advice for men with disabilities. The website for Selective Service advises, "Men who have a disability and who live at home must register with Selective Service if they can reasonably leave their homes and move about independently. A friend or relative may help a disabled man fill out the registration form if he can't do it himself.... men with disabilities that would disqualify them from military service still must register with Selective Service."

The site goes on to explain that should another draft ever be enacted, upon examination, a disqualifying disability would be elicit deferment, and sufficient documentation of that disability can get deferment without the examination, but registry is still mandatory unless the man is confined to the home or an institution due to his disability.

In other words, if you can go sit on a park bench every day and watch the world go by, Uncle Sam wants a chance to get a good look at you before determining whether you can be exempt from the draft.

Then there is the crisis in care for disabled veterans, who face inconsistent or even lack of access, long wait times, abuse, neglect, and dehumanizing failure of consideration under the grievously mismanaged Veterans Health Administration system. This impacts both sexes, but the vast, overwhelming majority of combat veterans are men, and the disparity only widens with disability.

Women get government support for defending
themselves or for their families to defend them
against violence and other abuses. Men get
government-ordered to sign up to potentially be sent
into the most violent environment known to
humankind, only to be neglected or even outright
abused by the very system that sent them there, if
they return with disabling conditions.

That's not the only systematic, institutionalized
discrimination disabled men and boys face.

Feminism's history of attacks on due process rights
has also hit the disabled, and again, especially men
and boys, already disadvantaged in the criminal
justice system, as we have highlighted in past articles.

Additionally:

A 2015 report by the National Council on Disability
stated, "Studies show that up to 85 percent of youth in
juvenile detention facilities have disabilities that
make them eligible for special education services, yet
only 37 percent receive these services while in
school." Let me remind you, Justice Bureau statistics
show that 95% of incarcerated youth are boys.
The report goes on to say, "A disproportionate
percentage of these detained youth are youth of color.
These statistics should lead to the conclusion that
many disabled youth in the juvenile justice and
criminal justice systems are deprived of an
appropriate education that could have changed their
School-to-Prison Pipeline trajectory. The 'School-to-
Prison Pipeline' refers to policies and practices that
push our nation's school children, especially those
most at risk, out of classrooms and into the juvenile
and criminal justice systems. This pipeline reflects the
prioritization of incarceration over education."

The ACLU has reported on conflicts between police
officers and the deaf, who often get accused of
resisting for failing to follow instructions they could
not hear, and which therefore were not actually
communicated to them.

Disability can lead to a person failing to understand officers' instructions or commands, charges leveled against him, the nature and scope of his defense options, his attorney's advice, questions he is asked in court, and how to explain innocent but abnormal behaviors or conditions, or adverse experiences, without falsely incriminating himself in the eyes of police, court personnel, judges, and jury members. He may be unconvincing when telling the truth, easily tripped up or falsely made to look dishonest or incompetent to tell the truth by authorities attempting to catch him in a lie or just to get another conviction under their belts. He may also be vulnerable to suggestion via pressure from authorities trying to get that conviction.

A 2016 report by RespectAbility.org states that there are 750,000 adults with disabilities behind bars. That number is Respect Ability's estimate based on Bureau of Justice statistics indicating that 32 percent of federal prisoners and 40 percent of people in jail have at least one disability. More than half a million of them have cognitive disabilities.

Justice Bureau data also reveals that the disabled are a disproportionately represented population in prison and jail settings. One survey found that about 32% of prisoners have at least one disability, as opposed to 11% of the general population. Another found that 40% percent of jail inmates have at least one disability, compared to 9% of those in the general population.

Prison inmates were 4 times as likely to report having a cognitive disability than the general population. Jail inmates were 6.5 times more likely. A higher percentage of incarcerated women than incarcerated men reported ambulatory and cognitive disabilities, but the overwhelming majority of incarcerated people are men, and in raw numbers, they report more of all disabilities. Further, reports also show that men are more likely to have a disability and not report it.

The problem, however, is not just in the area of wrongful conviction.

Respect Ability's report states that "Once individuals with a disability are in the system, they face significant problems including access to counsel, a lack of accommodations, complex rules, systematic abuse, and solitary confinement. Many are abused behind bars. For example, people who are deaf or blind are put in solitary for years as an "accommodation;" however, evidence shows that this can cause them to have significant mental health problems."

A 2017 report by the ACLU explains that prisoners in solitary confinement, a punishment reserved almost uniquely for men and boys, are often required by correctional facilities "to go without the devices, services, and treatment they need to perform basic human functions and remain healthy" while they are "held in small cells for 22 hours a day or longer, for days, months, and even years."

After being consistently failed by their schools, law enforcement, and the courts, incarcerated disabled convicts routinely face abuse, exploitation, and neglect that would land any other professionals responsible for their welfare jail themselves. The ACLU's report, "Caged In: The Devastating Harms of Solitary Confinement on Prisoners with Physical Disabilities" describes "people with disabilities - mental and physical - left to languish in despair, isolated, shut off, and prohibited from gaining equal access to programs and services," and "at serious risk of physical and psychological harm, especially in those facilities that are overcrowded or understaffed."

The report highlights several areas of mismanagement and misconduct which lead to egregious treatment of disabled inmates, including decrepit and unsanitary living conditions, lack of access to health care, failure of facility staff to prevent violence perpetrated against disabled inmates by other inmates, and environments which exacerbate symptoms experienced by inmates with psychiatric conditions in ways that lead to them receiving more punishment.

The ACLU's recommendations for reforms to end
these deplorable conditions and the heinous treatment
of America's disabled inmates include the suggestion
that institutions which house disabled prisoners
should comply with the Americans with Disabilities
act in terms of accessible design, inmate access to
proper equipment, care, and assistance, and
rehabilitative programs. They literally had to suggest
that U.S. government-run or funded facilities for
penalizing criminal offenders should not violate
federal law.

Let that sink in a moment while you remember that
when we've previously discussed the prison system,
we pointed out that feminist organizations have been
fighting to replace incarceration of female convicts
(and only female convicts) with rehabilitative
therapy. If the Women's March wants to do
something no other feminist organization deserves
credit for doing, they should expand that advocacy to,
at the very least, disabled inmates of both sexes. Or
perhaps, they should not push for due process
violations that would so severely disadvantage that
population in the first place.

What do you think? Should we hold our breath and
wait for that to happen?

Sources:

Wheelchairs, Braille Materials, Hearing Aids, And
Other Vital Devices Are Often Denied In Solitary

<u>Disability and Criminal Justice Reform: Keys to Success</u>

<u>Disabilities Among Prison and Jail Inmates, 2011–12</u>

<u>Promoting Justice for Men with Disabilities</u>

<u>Disability Rights Education & Defense Fund: School-to-Prison Pipeline</u>

<u>Breaking the School-to-Prison Pipeline for Students with Disabilities</u>

<u>TIME, Human Rights Watch ignore male victims of violence, report that female victims are ignored</u>

<u>CAGED IN: Solitary Confinement's Devastating Harm on Prisoners With Physical Disabilities</u>

<u>FFF: Veteran's Day 2015: Nov. 11, 2015</u>

<u>Eugenics:</u>

<u>Feminism and Eugenics in Germany and Britain, 1900-1940: A Comparative Perspective</u>

<u>Abortion, Eugenics and the Meaning of Margaret Sanger</u>

<u>Black Genocide</u>

<u>Eugenic feminism</u>

Disabilities among the incarcerated:

Part 2: The Supercrip

Throughout history men with disabilities have reached the heights of human achievement in personal and cultural terms, and they did so without the help of social justice warriors or modern reforms to laws, community access, or improved social attitudes toward disability.

Think of the presidents, artists, scientists, blade runners and the Everest-scaling amputees who reached for greatness, along with their less visible counterparts who went about their daily lives in less grandiose but nevertheless competent ways while living with a disability.

Disability always poses limitations on a person's physical or mental abilities, but the disability never encompasses the entire person – there remain competencies that deserve equal recognition in the mix.

Said differently a person is never completely disabled, just as there is no such thing as a person without a disability, however mild; eg. asthma, eczema, or gluten allergy can likewise interfere with daily functioning, forcing you to buy special creams and soaps or having to skip lunch with friends because you can't eat the food at that restaurant.

A study of high achievers illustrates the point of competency existing alongside disability. Franklin D. Roosevelt had post-polio paralysis, Ray Charles was blind, Christopher Reeve had a spinal injury, George Washington had dyslexia, Ludwig van Beethoven went deaf, Albert Einstein had Aspergers, Leonardo Da Vinci was epileptic, and the cosmologist Stephen Hawking has advanced motor neurone disease. Yet all of these men reached the top of their fields of interest.

Admiration of such men is today frowned upon by social justice warriors (SJWs) who believe the achievements misrepresent the common man with a disability and lead him to feel inferior by comparison. Referred to disparagingly as "supercrips" (super cripples), SJWs disparage high achievers as tall poppies who disrupt the level playing field, traitors who promote **ableism** instead of accepting their lot as sufferers without talents or abilities.

In a more reasonable use of the term, supercrip is sometimes employed as a reference to fanciful caricatures; eg. exaggerated claims about men on the autism spectrum as genius savants; or that the deaf have the sight of an eagle; or that the blind possess sonic radar abilities like dolphins or bats that help them move around the physical environment. There is no doubt, however, that the supercrip slur is also aimed at men with disabilities who genuinely achieved great things, but who are perceived as succeeding due to an unfair degree of male privilege.

Sound familiar? Most would have heard this criticism before, after 50 years of feminism's attempts to tear down every man who has had the drive and discipline to reach the top of his field. Even our disabled heroes are not spared by feminists who refer to them as 'privileged by patriarchy' and thus less handicapped than disabled women:

> "It will be argued in this paper that disability is a more severely handicapping condition for women than for men… [men] are relatively advantaged in that they can observe and may aspire to the advantaged place of males in today's society. Women with disabilities are perceived as inadequate to fulfill either the economically productive roles traditionally considered appropriate for males.

> "In research conducted by Mauer disabled females were more likely than disabled males to identify with a disabled storybook character; the disabled males were more likely to identify with the able-bodied character (1979). Disabled men may have a choice between a role of advantage (male) and a role of disadvantage (disability). Their decision is frequently a strategic identification with males.[1]

Feminist scholars refer to this as a 'double disadvantage' experienced by disabled women because they suffer from both disability and sexism, while their male counterparts are presumably being served up with caviar in their patriarchally privileged, gold-plated wheelchairs. Referring to the intersectional model, many feminists would go further and talk of multiple disadvantages such as triple, quadruple, or quintuple handicaps as would be the case for a black, transgendered, albino woman with a disability….. but I digress.

Indeed, a survey of feminist-inspired literature reveals a disturbing emphasis on what is *lacking* in comparison to what is good in the lives of disabled individuals, with that fixation coming at the expense of recognizing the multiple competencies or abilities that disabled individuals might possess. Moreover, the practice of gender stereotyping obscures the uniqueness of the individual, as underscored by sociologist Tom Shakespeare who states, "Disabled people's gender identity is more complex and more varied than this stereotypical view indicates. Some women feel liberated from social expectation as a result of impairment; some men feel doubly inferior."[2]

The double-disadvantage meme has led to the widespread view that disabled men gain privilege at women's expense, an advantage apparently in need of restricting in order to give disabled women a head start. In order to bring women forward we are led to believe we must push men back and downplay their extraordinary achievements.

Ridding the world of tall poppies, however, results in having no one to look up to. It forces us to lower our vision to a mean-average of attainment where social justice warriors seem bent on placing us – including those with disabilities. Some of us may be content with day-to-day existing and are not interested in pushing our personal limits, but there are others who want more. By honoring the achievements of exceptional people we understand a greater range of possibility, and can set our goals as high as we choose.

References

[1] Michelle Fine, 'Disabled women: Sexism Without the Pedestal' *Journal of Sociology and Social Welfare* (1977)
[2] Tom Shakespeare, 'When is a man not a man? When he's disabled,' in Working with Men for Change, p.49 (1999)

Feature image of Stephen Hawking by Lwp Kommunikáció

Part 3:
Institutional gynocentrism

As with parenting and school education, the disability
sector is overwhelmingly managed and staffed by
women. They are the nurses, community support
workers, personal care assistants, physiotherapists,
guidance counselors and so on. That domination
ensures women's views about gender govern the
provision of services for most disabled men. Before
discussing the problems created by this skewed
situation, let's begin with a look at the rise of the
disability rights movement.

Although disability issues received varying levels of
attention throughout history, they became an
international *cause célèbre* from 1960s, this on the
tail of the black civil rights movement in America,
and coinciding with the rise of second wave
feminism. This generated nothing short of a
revolution in awareness about the lives and needs of
people with disabilities.

The disability rights movement helped to secure
greater access to the social and physical environment,
as well as opportunities for independent living,
employment, education, and housing. It also
promoted freedom from abuse, neglect, and other
violations, and the establishment of civil rights
legislation to secure these opportunities and rights.

So far so good. However in recent years the movement has suffered mission-creep into the arena of gender politics. We are now more likely to hear about domestic violence and sexual assault against disabled women, their wage discrimination and other forms of double-disadvantage, while contrasting them with the depravity, privilege, rapiness and violence-proneness of disabled men — a narrative fostering denial of vulnerabilities men may face along with a demonizing of men to boot.

It's a growing problem that needs to be addressed.

I'm not suggesting we should stop paying attention to issues like sexual assault and abuse against women, which absolutely *must* be addressed for this vulnerable demographic. But we needn't demonize men and boys as the default perpetrator class, nor discriminate against them which we do by refusing to recognize males as victims of abuse and by dismissing or silencing those who might speak about it.

I know dozens of disabled men who have suffered serious violence or sexual abuse who have been afraid to tell someone for fear of being disbelieved, blamed or ridiculed. Marginalizing the issues of disabled men in the service of a one-sided gendered approach ultimately undermines the good work of the disability rights movement during the last 50 years – it shifts the focus from a humanitarian movement to a largely sexist one from within its own culture.

The gynocentric approach is compounded by the fact that most workers in the sector are women, who understandably have a more empathic appreciation of women's concerns than men's. The existence of female bias in the disability sector can be stressed in the following way: *many women possess an inadequate understanding of the experiences and concerns of men with disabilities.*

Poorly educated female workers, ie. those providing most of the frontline services, tend to rely on male stereotypes to guide their understandings of clientele, imposing the usual boilerplate images of males as utilitarian, rough, insensitive, sport obsessed, sex-obsessed, and so on. That vision is devoid of deeper knowledge of men generally, is at variance to the *individuality* of males specifically, and it tends to dictate the tone of care.

At this point readers may feel I'm being a little hard on female disability workers, which is correct. More accurately I'm being hard on the current *culture* of disability services because of the growing gynocentric trend, and pointing to an area of potential improvement in service provision. To be fair, I have no hesitation in admitting the existence of excellent female disability workers who do understand men's issues and provide a very high quality of support, but these are more often the exception rather than the rule. This article however is attempting to show where disability services are failing in their duty of care for men, and the increasing gynocentric culture is, at least to my thinking, the area of greatest failure.

Having worked in the disability field for 30 years, I've had more opportunity than most to observe the provision of services to men. The following are six areas where gender stereotyping is failing men with disabilities.

1. Men do, women are

In a recent article I described how men are considered utilities or 'action men' expected to be of service to others.[1] The expectation is sadly no different for disabled men, and one of the first things female support workers often do is put him to work doing odd jobs and showing him how to be 'useful' to women and society. A woman with an identical disability will often get asked a different set of questions – like what do you want to do to have fun.

2. Male aggression or violence is an attempt to dominate

Both men and women with disabilities sometimes times find life frustrating and lash out in anger. Typically males are lectured about how their aggression upsets other people, causes damage to the wider world, and are instructed on how to control their anger – while the disabled woman who lashes out in the same manner is calmed and asked what or who is bothering her and perhaps how the world might be rearranged so that it doesn't upset her again. Disability support workers are less likely to consider the real distress or *powerlessness* that causes men to lash out.

3. Males are rarely victims of violence

Government media campaigns focusing solely on "violence against women" have encouraged the assumption that men are default perpetrators who don't suffer violence. The belief among support workers that disabled men are safe from violence has created an environment in which abused men are less likely to speak up and seek help… there is no encouragement to do otherwise. Despite the fact that U.S. Department of Justice has reported violence crimes against disabled men and women at roughly equal rates,[2] a Google search for information delivers the following disparity of awareness:

▶ "Violence against disabled women" = 4330 results.
▶ "Violence against disabled men" = 9 results.

4. Males are unlikely to suffer sexual abuse or rape

As with men in prisons who experience high levels of sexual assault, disabled males are four times more likely than nondisabled men to be sexually assaulted or raped.[3] The researchers of that study found that more than 5 percent of disabled men reported experiencing sexual assault during the past year, about equal to sexual assaults against disabled women.[3]

If 'rape culture' is based in social invisibility and voicelessness of a victim group, then disabled men are dealing with a legitimate rape culture – one entrenched by the people who receive a weekly pay-cheque to help lift that silence. Again a Google search speaks volumes:

▶ "Sexual violence against disabled women" = 1520 results.
▶ "Sexual violence against disabled men" = 0 results.

5. Men are less in need of assistance than women

As addressed in part one, disabled men are deemed privileged by patriarchy while women with disabilities are considered doubly disadvantaged by the same. The gynocentric privileges historically afforded to women have not yet entered the discourse – such as being recipients of living expenses drawn from male labor, or receiving greater provision and protection generally. Gynocentric prioritization is further underlined in phrases like "damsel in distress," "ladies before gentlemen," "girls before boys" or "ladies first,", which are codes of chivalric and gentlemanly behavior that place disabled men in second place on the basis of their sex.

The stereotype of the cigar-smoking, brandy swilling patriarch, in combination with the custom of "ladies first," sees that men are at a disadvantage to women in the fight for limited disability services.

6. Male sexual needs are socially unacceptable

Men's sexual desires are gross and in need of suppressing or civilizing, so think some individuals charged with supporting men with disabilities. Cultural narratives characterizing male sexuality as dirty, violent and oppressive are clearly toxic to male self-image, however some among the mostly female workforce have adopted that negative mindset and with it created barriers to men's attempts to enjoy healthy sexual expression.

When a disabled man desires a woman, or
masturbates, or perhaps decides to hire a prostitute –
all natural behaviors – female support workers tend to
be unsupportive, believing sexual desires must be
tamed in the service of something more civilized such
as nonsexual dating and romantic love.

I have observed female staff match-make male and
female clientele — treating them like Barbie & Ken
in a child's dolls house — while also instructing men
in the arts of non-sexual chivalry, such as bringing
gifts and flowers for a potential girlfriend or perhaps
taking her to a romantic restaurant while the support
worker plays hostess. While perhaps well meaning,
my reading of such intervention is that it leaves out
many aspects of male nature, especially male sexual
needs, in favor of gynocentric themes which is
ultimately an insult to the men in question.

These are just a few examples of biases men with
disabilities face. Problems generated by gynocentrism
and misandry within the disability sector (and
beyond) are sometimes blatant and at other times
subtle, but in either case they are mostly
unrecognized and unquestioned by those on the front
lines of service provision.

Men with disabilities receive little more empathy than their able-bodied counterparts – and in some respects they receive less. As with all men's issues, from health funding to prostate cancer, birth control options, or homelessness, men are going to have to speak up – in fact they are going to have to shout up. Those in power might not see men's pain, but they will hear men's anger.

This leads to the next article in this series where we will look at a new kind of man with a disability – he is the one who says "No" to gynocentrism and other forms of mistreatment, and acts decisively to shut them down.

References

[1] Peter Wright, Don't just do something, SIT THERE (June 2015)
[2] Harrell, E., Rand, M., Crime Against People with Disabilities, U.S. Department of Justice (2008)
[3] Mitra, Monika, Vera E. Mouradian, and Marci Diamond. Sexual Violence Victimization Against Men with Disabilities, American Journal of Preventive Medicine (2011)

Feature image: Cpl. Anthony McDaniel

Part 4: Self-respect

In part one of this series we looked at men with disabilities who achieved greatness. In part two we looked at an emerging culture of gynocentrism in the disability sector, along with the impoverished and at times hostile "support" extended to men in need of assistance. In this third and final part we look at a new kind of man with a disability – a man who says "No" to bigotry and other forms of mistreatment, and who gears his life toward the cultivation of self-respect.

To illustrate this new kind of man we will turn to the Greek myth of the goddess Hera and her disabled son Hephaestus – a son who has to challenge his mother's ableism and bigotry before he can take his rightful place in the Olympian society. In this myth Hephaestus plays a role not unlike the hero Perseus who must stop Medusa's hostilities before men can go about their lives again in safety and dignity.

The son of Hera and Zeus, Hephaestus was born parthenogenically – ie. from Hera alone and not from the result of a sex act with Zeus. We are told that she planed to give birth to a son after Zeus went and gave birth to Bright Eyed Athena who became a golden child of the gods. Hera was incensed that Zeus would give birth to Athena without her sexual aid, and her creation of Hephaestus was carried out in revenge. Hera's message was essentially "You give birth without me, well I can do that too!"

Some myths suggest her son was born disabled, and others say he became disabled after his mother (or father) threw him from Mt. Olympus whereupon he landed hard on the earth and damaged his legs. In any case the dominant legend is that Hera gave birth to him already disabled, for which she was mightily disgusted in his lack of perfection.

Hera was angry and spoke thus among the assembled gods:

"Hear from me, all gods and goddesses… my son Hephaestus whom I bore was weakly among all the blessed gods and shrivelled of foot, a shame and a disgrace to me in heaven, whom I myself took in my hands and cast out so that he fell in the great sea. But silver-shod Thetis the daughter of Nereus took and cared for him with her sisters: would that she had done other service to the blessed gods!"[1]

[Above: While Zeus reaches out to his daughter Athena, Hera ejects her disabled son from Olympus – circa 200-150 B.C.]

Hera was ashamed of her son's disability, one which caused him to limp on both feet since the soles and heels were turned back to front and were not fitted for walking but only for a forward-rolling motion of the whole body.[4] This 'difference' made Hephaestus a fringe person on Olympus, and threatened to put his mother on the fringes too, so she hid the secret by throwing her son to what she assumed would be his death. Fortunately he was saved by some kindly goddesses who nurtured him back to health.

After his fall from the heavens Hephaestus grew up on a secluded island and there learned the art of blacksmithing. He devoted himself to the task with such discipline that his artisan skills became the finest in the world. Despite the pride he took in these achievements he would not forget the cruel treatment of Hera who dismissed him as ugly and lacking in usefulness. Like so many men today who wish to be seen as something other than utilities for women and society, Hephaestus remains angry;

Hephaestus says: "Thetis saved me when I suffered much at the time of my great fall through the will of my own brazen-faced mother, who wanted to hide me for being lame. Then my soul would have taken much suffering had not Eurynome and Thetis caught me and held me… With them I worked nine years as a smith, and wrought many intricate things; pins that bend back, curved clasps, cups, necklaces, working there in the hollow of the cave, and the stream of Okeanos around us went on forever with its foam and its murmur." [2]

Classical sociologist Philip Slater suggests that Hera despises her son's masculinity and his disability, preferring instead to have a son of heroic proportions who could provide her with utility and glory. Hera's attitude provokes, in later myths, a kind of self-abasing buffoonery from Hephaestus that Slater interprets as "an appropriate response to his mother's narcissistic resentment of males–she cannot deflate him if he is already deflated–but it is therefore all the more inappropriate for dealing with her *contrary* desire for him to be a display piece and an agent for the expression of her masculine strivings. It is for this reason, after all, that she threw him down from Olympus."[3]

Like Hephaestus, many men with disabilities are angry. They realize that they are being doubly marginalized due to the curse of having a penis yet being unable, or perhaps unwilling, to perform as utilities for women and society – they know they are being negatively judged for it.

In her mythos Hera provides the quintessential example of gynocentric feminism, along with ableist and misandrist attitudes to boot. Her attitude represents much that is wrong with the disability sector today – an underlying bigotry that men must reject if they are to enjoy freedom, dignity and self-respect.

Challenging that bigotry is precisely what Hephaestus does. He gains redress against Hera for rejecting him by making her a magical golden throne which, when she sat on it, did not allow her to stand up. None of the other gods could release her and they begged Hephaestus to return to Olympus to let his mother go, but he refused, saying "I have no mother."[4]

The gods were impressed with his rebuke of Hera and agree accept him back into Olympian society as one of their own. This may be viewed as a positive reappraisal of his disability – Hephaestus possesses previously unrecognized skills, is sharp of mind, humbles Hera, and is accepted by the other Olympians. Here is a synopsis of the story thus far;

> After his abandonment, Thetis found him and took him to her underwater grotto and raised him as her own son.

> Hephaestus had a happy childhood with dolphins as his playmates and pearls as his toys. Late in his childhood, he found the remains of a fisherman's fire on the beach and became fascinated with an unextinguished coal, still red-hot and glowing.

Hephaestus carefully shut this precious coal in a clamshell, took it back to his underwater grotto, and made a fire with it. On the first day after that, Hephaestus stared at this fire for hours on end. On the second day, he discovered that when he made the fire hotter with bellows, certain stones sweated iron, silver or gold. On the third day he beat the cooled metal into shapes: bracelets, chains, swords and shields. Hephaestus made pearl-handled knives and spoons for his foster mother, and for himself he made a silver chariot with bridles so that seahorses could transport him quickly. He even made slave-girls of gold to wait on him and do his bidding.

Later, Thetis left her underwater grotto to attend a dinner party on Mount Olympus wearing a beautiful necklace of silver and sapphires that Hephaestus had made for her. Hera admired the necklace and asked where she could get one. Thetis became flustered, causing Hera to become suspicious; and, at last, the queen god discovered the truth: the baby she had once rejected had grown into a talented blacksmith.

Hera was furious and demanded that Hephaestus return home, a demand that he refused. However he did send Hera a beautifully constructed chair made of silver and gold, inlaid with mother-of-pearl. Hera was delighted with this gift but, as soon as she sat in it her weight triggered hidden springs and metal bands sprung forth to hold her fast. The more she shrieked and struggled the more firmly the mechanical throne gripped her; the chair was a cleverly designed trap.

For three days Hera sat fuming, still trapped in Hephaestus's chair; she could not sleep, she could not stretch, she could not eat. It was Zeus who finally saved the day: he promised that if Hephaestus released Hera he would give him a wife, Aphrodite the goddess of love and beauty. Hephaestus agreed and married Aphrodite.[5]

After his mother rejects him for having a mobility impairment he becomes angry and he ensures that *her* mobility is impaired by trapping her in a throne. The gesture can be read as forcing Hera to experience a mobility challenge that she seemed utterly unable or unwilling to sympathize with.

Commenting on the story, disability advocate William Ebenstein states;

"In the Hephaestus myth we can discern a
positive psychology of anger that is grounded
in the experience of disability. The disabled
deity refuses to play the role of the passive
victim. Instead he is an active creator in
forging his future place in society.
Hephaestus' revenge is accomplished in such
a clever and artful way that, in the end, it is
enriching for the entire Olympian
community."

"In Hephaestus we find a character who is
motivated by his anger to confront a world
that has discarded him. He stages what
amounts to a non-violent demonstration, an
act of civil disobedience that completely shuts
down Olympus. His stubborn anger does not
lead to acceptance, adjustment or passivity.
On the contrary it lifts him up to reclaim his
dignity and civil rights. The story depicts a
community that must adjust to someone who
has been stigmatized, segregated, and
discriminated against. It is the disabled
character himself who creates the humorous
situation as an effective tool to confront his
oppression and challenge the existing order."[6]

Hephaestus' anger energizes his expression of outrage in place of squashing it as a male character flaw. The problems he sees *are in the world* and Hephaestus takes action there, where it counts. His demonstration of outrage in response to an ugly world, or over acts of mistreatment, is mental health at its finest and similar expression needs to be encouraged and supported for all people with disabilities. In fact, speaking out of one's anger is a perfect example of what is intended by the disability-related term self-advocacy.

Like our mythical protagonist, the 'Hephaestus man' understands where the problem lies and will not have his concerns silenced.

Too often we see psychotherapists and rehabilitation counsellors engage in gender stereotyping, viewing positive anger as 'male aggression,' 'patriarchy,' or 'toxic masculinity' that in disabled and nondisabled men supposedly needs correcting. However killing the outrage is a misandric move, one that leads to a loss of personal agency in the world for men.

Thus far Hephaestus' story has been one of rejection and redress. However the story is far more than a one-dimensional recounting of an "angrycrip" who ends up exacting revenge against his tormentors. It involves the larger vision of forging self-respect, the beginnings of which were long stirring before he sought to challenge the ableist culture among the gods.

Following his story from beginning to end we see the goal of self-respect is something Hephaestus cultivates quite independently from the respect he has won from the gods.[7] After rejoining the Olympian hierarchy as dignified contributor – craftsman of the gods – he continues the inner work he started as a child when he located value *in his own eyes*, and not in the shallow eyes of others.

The key principle, one given in an incisive article by Paul Elam, is "self-respect isn't earned, it's taken."[8] When Hephaestus engages with the Olympian community, he doesn't need to wait around for their validation, he has already wrested it by his own self-assessment.

The Hephaestus man is the one who expresses his outrage at offensive behavior, and who chooses to cultivate self-respect. By respecting himself and demanding the same from others, Hephaestus demonstrates exactly what these things mean for men in today's world, disabled or not.

References

[1] Evelyn-White translation, Homeric Hymn to Pythian Apollo (1914)
[2] Richmond Lattimore translation, The Iliad by Homer (1951)
[3] Philip E. Slater, The Glory of Hera: Greek Mythology and The Greek Family (1968)
[4] Karl Kerenyi, The Gods of the Greeks, pp.155-158 (1951)

[5] Wikipedia, Greek myths of Hephaestus, (Roman name Vulcan changed to Hephaestus above)
[6] William Ebenstein, Toward an Archetypal Psychology of Disability Based on the Hephaestus Myth (2006)
[7] Murray Stein, Hephaistos: A pattern of introversion, in The Selected Works of Murray Stein (1973).
[8] Paul Elam, Self-respect isn't earned, it's taken (2015)

About the authors:

Peter Wright and Hannah Wallen are qualified professionals working in the disability sectors in the USA and Australia respectively. Their combined experience in the field spans more than 50 years.